Len Lester

And lately, by the Tavern Door agape,
Came stealing through the Dusk an Angel Shape
　　Bearing a Vessel on his shoulder; and
He bid me taste of it; and 'twas—the Grape!

The Rubáiyát of Omar Khayyám

THE CRAFT OF MAKING WINE

designed, written, and illustrated by

Jan Adkins

advisors:

David Dionne, the country wines

David Hottenstein, the grape wines

Printed in the United States of America

First published in the United States of America
by the Walker Publishing Company, Incorporated.
Published simultaneously in Canada by
Fitzhenry and Whiteside, Ltd.

Library of Congress catalogue card number: 75-161106
ISBN: 0-8027-0359-3

This book is dedicated to Sam Walker

Grace Darling Griffin

William B. Decker

and to my friends at Walker and Confused Company
including an unlikely leprechaun;
they believe in print and in people.

HEREIN:

Preface	8
The Families of Wine	11
White	12
Rosé	13
Red	14
Country	15
Flower	16
Sparkling	17
What Is Good Wine?	18
Tasting	19
What will you need?	20
Tools	21
Chemistry of Ferment	22
Raw Materials	24
Crusher	28
Press	29
Crocks	30
Vessels	31
Fermentation Locks	32
Hydrometer	34
✠ *Hydrometer Tables*	36
Sulfur Dioxide	37
Yeast	38
Chemicals	40
Bottles	42
Corks	44
Corkers	44
Miscellaneous	46

The Making of a Red Wine   47

    Buying Grapes   48

    Starter Bottle   49

    Washing   50

    Crushing   51

    Hydrometer Testing   52

    Adding Sugar and Yeast   53

    Aerobic Fermentation   54

    Pressing   55

    Anaerobic Fermentation   56

    Stirring Lees   57

    Racking   58

    Topping Off   59

    Racking and Bottling   60

    Corking   61

    Storing and Sampling   62

    Resumé   63

White Wine   64

    Crushing/Pressing   65

    Amelioration   66

    Oxidation and Temperature   67

    Clearing   68

    Filtering   69

Rosé Wines   70

The Country Wines   72

    Cider   76

Flower Wines   78

Concentrates   80

Sparkling Wines   82

Corkscrews   84

Legality   86

Access   88

index   90

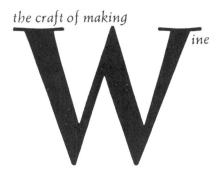

the craft of making

Wine

Giants were in the earth, then, and man still had some dominion over the fish of the sea, the fowl of the air, and the beasts of a world still warm from creation. Language was yet a bulky problem, heretic tigers regularly ate passers-by, a proper system for waterproofing a cave lay dismally undeveloped, such women and song as were available seemed incomplete, something was lacking. The world spread new and rough—its corners needed rounding.

In the dim parts of a cave, a clay jug full of fruit juice stoppered with a muddy stick sat forgotten. Inside it, dark and airless, decay had its natural way . . . and a bubble rose to the surface! There was no fanfare (there was no trumpet), but the occasion deserved it, because when the cave's owner investigated a loud pop and the source of a flying muddy stick, he found substance that has benefited, plagued, obsessed, calmed, revived, and sustained men and nations through all the time since. He found a darkly clear juice tart and sweet with the alcohols and sugars of ferment, fragrant with the smell of fruit, cool in the mouth, warm in the stomach. He tasted it and he thought it was good—but he had never tasted a Premier Grand Crux.

Wine goes far back. Even our word for it goes back past history in a singularly direct etymology: back to the Middle English *win*, back to Old English *wine* and Old High German *win*, further back to Germanic and Early Latin *vinum*, further to Greek *oinos*, further still and the origins fade into prehistory, not even from the first stock of Indo-European syllables, as far back as its use and esteem.

It is something more than a beverage: clean and lasting, safe and healthful, nourishing and refreshing, relaxing, even subduing—it is more than that. Wrought gold, smooth silver, and gemstones, all the most cherished prizes of a people find their way into the rituals of state and holiness. Precious metals, fragrant woods, rich weaves, and—always—wine. In some way wine touches the deep roots of man; there is beauty in it.

We know that grapes were cultivated for winemaking by the Assyrians and Egyptians around 3500 B.C. The Pharaohs included the cuttings for a vineyard in the cargo of their death boats. Around 500 B.C. Phoenician traders brought grapevine roots to Greece: They were well received; the gods were delighted. Amphora filled with Greek wine (slightly past its prime) are still returned to the surface from Greek gallies that foundered twenty-five hundred years ago.

9

The Romans, too, poured out a little of their winecup for the Romanized gods and planted their hills in vineyards still growing today. The gods' festivals were sure profit for the wine trader, and wine played central roles in the ritual (and the fervor) of the secret cults. The Bacchanalian cult of Dionysus leaned heavily on wine's release of inhibitions for its racy demeanor, and the early Christian cults (competing with the Dionysians for converts) adopted wine as their sacrament in doses rather more generous than are dispensed today.

Through the slow decay of the Empire, monasteries vinted their own wines, keeping the art of the grape intact for the awakening of Europe and the huge output of the Renaissance vintners. Dom Perignon, a French monk around 1700, began the use of corks (instead of tarred cloth) and invented champagne. European vines followed explorers into the New World by only twenty-five years when Cortez ordered a cargo of Spanish vines to Mexico. The vines adapted, flourished, and traveled with the Jesuit fathers to the California valleys.

Every country has its ferment, its grapes, and seasons. The major wine-making countries are mostly stepchildren of European vines: from France, Italy, Germany, Spain, and Portugal, to Argentina, Russia, Algeria, and the United States. Almost 85 per cent of contemporary European vines, however, have been nourished by American roots since phylloxera, a root-burrowing louse, spread to European vines from ingrate American vines planted experimentally in Europe at the turn of the century. Phylloxera spread epidemically until horticulturists levied stringent transport restrictions on the continent and grafted phylloxera-resistant American native roots to the dying European vines. The plan was drastic and successful; the vineyards of Europe produce more wine than ever before.

THE FAMILIES OF WINE

White
Rosé
Red
Country
Flower
Sparkling

WHITE WINES

A white wine is clear and light, with a refreshing taste and a fresh bouquet. White wines may be bracing and dry—even astringent, mild and gentle, discretely sweet. Their colors are exercises in subtlety, progressing quietly from springwater clarity to merest amber or a faint and distant green, and on into a golden warmth. White wine ferments from the juice of its fruit alone and does not lie with the skins of the grape to take on its coloring. This light taste does not subdue the delicate flavors of simply prepared fish and shellfish, mild cheeses, light pork and veal, or domestic poultry; generally, a white wine is served with a dish whose flavor must not be intimidated by a more robust taste.

ROSÉ WINES

Rosé is a gay wine, the happy stepbrother of the white wines. Its spectrum ranges from a racy blush to an excited pink, a festive crowd of lucid, high-chroma colors. It has had a brief affair with the skins of its fruit, having lain with them for a matter of hours or days to acquire the right color and a subtle shift in taste, a slightly higher body. Rosé is a congenial wine, complimenting a great variety of foods, especially pleasant with cold foods, and possibly excluding only desserts, very oily foods, and overpowering flavors. It flatters any table.

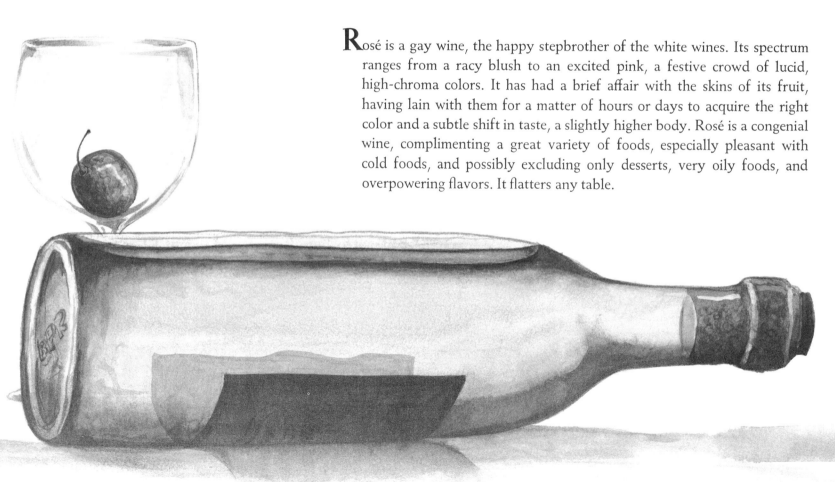

RED WINES

Red wine is a male concept: It is rich and imposing, assertive; it has a presence. It is full-bodied and commands a pronounced taste that cleanses, a big bouquet, and a true depth of color. Red wine ferments with the skins of its fruit, assuming pigment and the hearty bite of peel. It is a partner to red meat, to steaks and chops and joints of beef and lamb. It contends beautifully with the piquant flavor of game or rich cheese, and accords itself with roast geese and ducks, as the edge of its taste cuts through the oil of a fatty food and leaves the palate clean.

The country wines are made from almost every fruit except grapes: elderberries, raspberries, apples, strawberries, plums, peaches. Nearly every fruit (or vegetable) with sugar to ferment and an acid base can be the basis for a country wine. Prime wine grapes are not available everywhere, so the fruit wines are popular with some winemakers. Their colors, tastes, bouquets, and strengths vary greatly, but the winemaking processes are unchanged.

COUNTRY WINES

FLOWER WINES

The flower wines hold a slim but dainty claim to the title of wine, for while grapes and other fruits supply in some part the necessities for nourishing a wine, flowers afford only a delicate fragrance and a tiny flavor. Yet the fragrances and flavors are so unique that winemakers continue to blanch the petals of thousands of roses, dandelions, and marigolds, and add sugar, yeast, water, yeast nutrient, and endless patience to capture their fragile essence.

The winecrafter's art is to capture and blend days of sun, lifting winds, simple fruits, and the richness of the earth in bottles. With great skill and much labor, the vintner can even capture mirth and delight that leaps out of its bottle with an excited bang: champagne. Classically, champagne's pop is the product of a final ferment that builds carbon dioxide pressure within its strong and securely corked bottle, and its taste is the result of a blend from several grape varieties. Happiest as an apéritif or with dessert, champagne can accompany a wide range of foods, though it should be remembered that it is essentially a light, dry white wine. Sparkling Burgundy and Cold Duck (a sparkling blend of Burgundies and whites) happily fill a less classic but just as festive gustatory niche.

SPARKLING WINES

WHAT IS GOOD WINE?

A good wine is good to your eye, your nose, your mouth. A great wine is great to your eye, nose, and mouth. Beauty is in the eye, nose, and mouth of the beholder: You are the final authority on what is—to you—good wine. With bad luck and a hundred dollars you can buy a bad bottle of wine, a wine that does not please you. With good luck and a very small sum you can buy a wine that excites you and compliments your day. With luck and time and information, you can handcraft a wonderful wine.

To a limited extent, a taste for wine must be acquired. To educate the palate and nose to the exacting discrimination of a professional vintner is a life's project, perhaps the result of many generations' experience. Professional tasters may pronounce greatness for a wine, but there are so many kinds of wine, so many flavors and bouquets, that you may be unimpressed with the "great" wine, for the professional describes how near a vintage approaches the perfect qualities of its type: This Pinot Noir '65 is almost as good as any Pinot Noir could ever be. If sauerkraut experts proclaim a pot of sauerkraut to be as sauer and as kraut as any sauerkraut can be—a great sauerkraut—you may not like it, especially if you do not like sauerkraut.

Your preferences are your best guide, and your preferences will change as you taste more wines and become more acquainted with the types and years. A professional opinion may be very helpful still, in the choice between years or vintners of one type.

Wine is not beer; it is not quaffed. Wine is not brandy; it is not sipped. There is a technique for tasting wine.

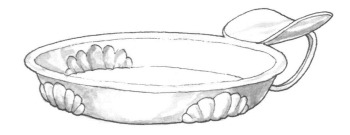

a silver tastevin *for sampling wine*

18

To taste the wine alone, you must cleanse your palate with a piece of white bread or mild cheese and perhaps a sip of water to make it ready for a new taste.

The sight of the wine is part of the taste. The body of the wine—the thickness of the fluid that shows itself as the tendency to curve up the walls of the glass —should indicate its substance; the color and clarity should delight the eye.

Now the bouquet, the wine's aroma. The wineglass you choose should be of adequate size (see Glasses, page 86) and tulip-shaped to concentrate the fragrant vapors above the wine. Swirl the wine and press your nose to the vapors; inhale and savor them, the essence of sun and fruit.

And the taste . . . a small mouthful rolled lightly on the tongue, caressing the hard palate, swallowed slowly, followed by a gentle inhalation to taste the bouquet. Tasting, you are on your own; the wine that tastes best to you is a great wine.

19

What will you need to produce a drinkable, pleasing wine?

Your initial cash outlay can be small, under $25 for equipment. Dependent on your location and the time of year, the price of grapes or juice or other fruit will vary. Of course, your investment can be much larger if you decide to purchase an array of wine tools, many of which you will probably acquire as your interest and expertise increase.

Space is an important consideration, not only working space for an occasionally messy job, but storage space that is quiet, dark, cool, and undisturbed. It will not do to disturb three months of settling and clearing to extract your snowshoes from under the wine vessel.

To make a wine you will need, most of all, patience. It will be six months or more before you can begin to pour out the fruit of your craft; the wine will require at least that time in fermenting and racking and clearing, to grow. Patience is a requisite of the careful washing and sterilizing your utensils must have, and of the culling, crushing, pressing, racking, and bottling. You will not be mixing chemicals to treat a lawn, but tending a living thing which hopes to appeal to your most sensitive senses; such things are done slowly and gently.

Carboy	$5
Hydrometer	3
Tubing	2
Corks	4
Lock	1
Corker	5
Chemicals	+3
	$23
Crusher	$40
Presser	$60

TOOLS

THE CHEMISTRY OF FERMENTATION

To know what you are about, you must understand in a general sense at least the alchemy that you work in changing fruit juice into wine: fermentation. Basically it is an anaerobic chemical rearrangement of organic compounds caused by microorganisms—that is, a process carried on in the absence of oxygen (anaerobic) which breaks down existing chemical compounds into their component parts by the action of microscopic yeast cells. The yeast acts especially on the sugars in your fruit juice, converting them to alcohol and carbon dioxide in parts roughly equal by weight, until the percentage of alcohol in the mixture is sufficient to destroy the yeast culture. When the yeast cells die, they no longer break down the chemical bonds, and fermentation stops.

The several factors that influence fermentation shape the wine itself.

Most important, of course, is the complex nature of the substance fermented. Not only the varying chemical makeup of varying kinds of fruit changes the taste and bouquet of wine; differing species of the same fruit color with their parts and proportions the flavor of a wine, and even the same species of the same fruit produces dissimilar wines when fermented at different stages in the fruit's development. Here, perhaps, is the line that separates science from art: Winemaking is not a mathematical certainty, never wholly predictable. Notably, the levels of sugars, acids, and mineral nutrients affect alcohol level and the body and dryness of the wine.

Yeast is a living culture of cells. The kind of yeast that carries on the ferment can affect the product (see Yeast, p. 38). Heat affects activity in the yeast culture: Warmth increases its activity until it begins to destroy the cells; cold slows down the process. Sunlight's ultraviolet rays can destroy a culture, so the fermentation must be kept well away from direct sunlight.

Fermentation can carry on without yeast. The sugars in fruit juice can be rearranged by bacteria, but the result is acetic acid (vinegar) rather than ethanol (the alcohol in wine). In either case, the by-product of fermentation is carbon dioxide, which must be allowed to escape while retaining the oxygen-free integrity of the ferment.

In general, then, the making of wine begins with a fruit juice and a yeast culture in a bacteria-free atmosphere sealed from outside oxygen by a water lock which allows carbon dioxide to escape under pressure and readmits no air.

RAW MATERIALS

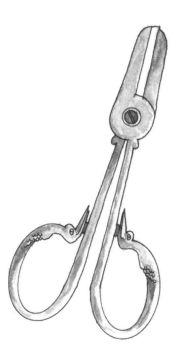

Best of all: the grape. Wines begin and end with the grape, a fruit cultured for beverage before history, supplying every need for proper ferment, the unsurpassed basis of winemaking. There are thousands of varieties of grapes and only a few dozen specially suited for vinting; some of them are listed here. A vineyard is the best place to buy grapes or, more conveniently, pressed juice. Farmers' markets supply grapes only in the vine regions. Wholesale produce markets may supply a few varieties in season, but consumer demand insists on the wine-worthless seedless and table varieties. Supermarkets only rarely offer a grape suitable for ferment.

Grape concentrates can produce an excellent table wine and can be shipped, usually in quantities yielding a five-gallon ferment, at any season of the year. Certainly something is lost in the dehydration, jugging, and packaging, but the concentrates make an even, acceptable wine.

Fruits for country wines can be gathered from the field or the supermarket, almost anywhere. Sprayed fruit should be carefully washed to flush away noxious chemical tastes.

Flowers for wine should be picked when the sun is up and the dew is off. Dandelions are surprisingly easy to cultivate.

Baco # 1	Inconsistent, usually a base for blends.
Barbera	Similar to a Chianti grape.
Cabernet Sauvignon	One of two best American reds, too fine for experimentation.
Carignane	Used extensively in concentrates.
Concord	Ameliorate to cut heavy taste, one part water to four parts juice; pick before fully ripe to preserve higher acid content; color and quality uncertain, varying with particular growth.
Couderc 4401	Unspectacular.
Foch	Inconsistent, usually a base for blends.
Gamay	Unspectacular.
Grenache	Primarily a rosé.
Gringnolino	Italian red.
Ives	Inconsistent and "foxy."
Petite Sirah	Fairly good red.
Pinot Noir	One of two best American reds, too fine for experimentation.
Norton	Native, well balanced, hard-to-find, the only American without "foxiness."
Ruby Sauvignon	Inferior to Cabernet Sauvignon.
Seibel 1000 5455 7053 13053	Good reds, varying with particular growth.
Seyve Villard	Unspectacular.
Tannat	Used in blending.
Zinfandel	Unspectacular.

RED GRAPES

This is by no means a complete list of the thousands of wine grape varieties.

Catawba	"Foxy," a good beginner's wine.
Chenin Blanc	Flowery, with a fruity bouquet.
Delaware	"Foxy," used in sparkling wines, a good beginner's wine; high in acid, ameliorate, one part water to four parts juice.
Dutchess	Good beginner's wine, less "foxy."
Folle Blanch	Thin white.
Grey Riesling (Grey Dutchess)	Light, fruity, not a true Riesling.
Niagara	Pronounced "foxiness," amelioration may help.
Norton	Native, well-balanced, hard-to-find, the only American without "foxiness."
Palomino	Ordinary white table wine, best for sherry.
Pinot Blanc	Good white.
Pinot Chardonnay	One of the best white wines; strong, lingering aftertaste.
Riesling Johannisberger	Light and fruity.
Sauvignon Blanc	Excellent white.
Sauvignon Vert	Poor.
Seibel 5279 9110	Good whites.
Sémillion	Excellent American sauterne, sweeter than French sauternes.
Seyval Blanc	Good white wine, especially for amateur.
Seyval Villard 5-247 12-375	Good whites.
Steuben	Good beginner's wine, less "foxy."
Sylvaner (Franken Riesling)	Light.
Traminer	Spicy.

WHITE GRAPES

FRUITS

The proportions of fruit to water given are approximates.

fruit	fruit/1 gallon water	remarks
Apples	20 pounds	This quantity is for apple wine; see page 76 for a thorough treatment of the cider process; add 3 tsps. citric acid.
Apricots	5 pounds	Remove stones, blanch and crush.
Blackberries	3 pounds	A difficult wine; add 2 tsps. citric acid.
Carrots	5 pounds	Boil chopped carrots in water until tender, remove carrots and use water.
Cherries	5 pounds	Crush (being especially careful not to break the stones) and blanch.
Crabapples	6 pounds	See apples above.
Dandelions	4 quarts blossoms	Pick blossoms in full bloom when the dew is gone; use petals only, measuring them as lightly pressed into container; blanch; add 3 tsps. citric acid.
Elderberries	2 pounds	Blanch; add 3 tsps. citric acid.
Peaches	6 pounds	Peaches were also used to make a preferred cider called "peachy," using the cider method described for apples; remove stones, blanch and crush.
Pears	4 pounds	Also used for cider, called "perry."
Plums	9 pounds	Remove stones, blanch and crush.
Raspberries	4 pounds	Blanch; add 2 tsps. citric acid.
Rosehips	12 ounces	Remove stalks and flower remains, cut in half and press or mince, blanch. Proportion refers to dried hips.
Strawberries	3 pounds	Blanch; add 2 tsps. citric acid.

A crusher is simply a bin feeding into the interlocking cogs of two rollers spaced at a distance that will break the skins but not crush the bitter seeds. Initially fermenting a red wine with the pulp, every skin must be broken, and an unbroken grape in the middle of a mass of grapes will withstand amazing pressures. Grapes are too precious to ignore any amount of juice. The crusher does a quick and complete job.

If a crusher is unavailable, fruit should be worked with the hands to break the skins. Traditionally, the winemaker and his friends could march around and around in the bathtub to the sound of a drum, treading out the grapes and staining feet, legs, tub, and floor an indelible red. The crusher is most efficient, and hands are next best, but the tub and drum have a certain wild charm.

CRUSHER

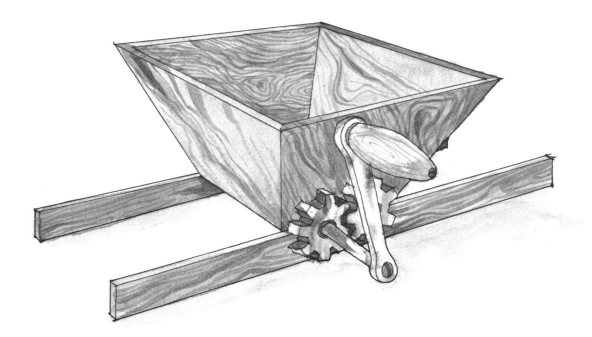

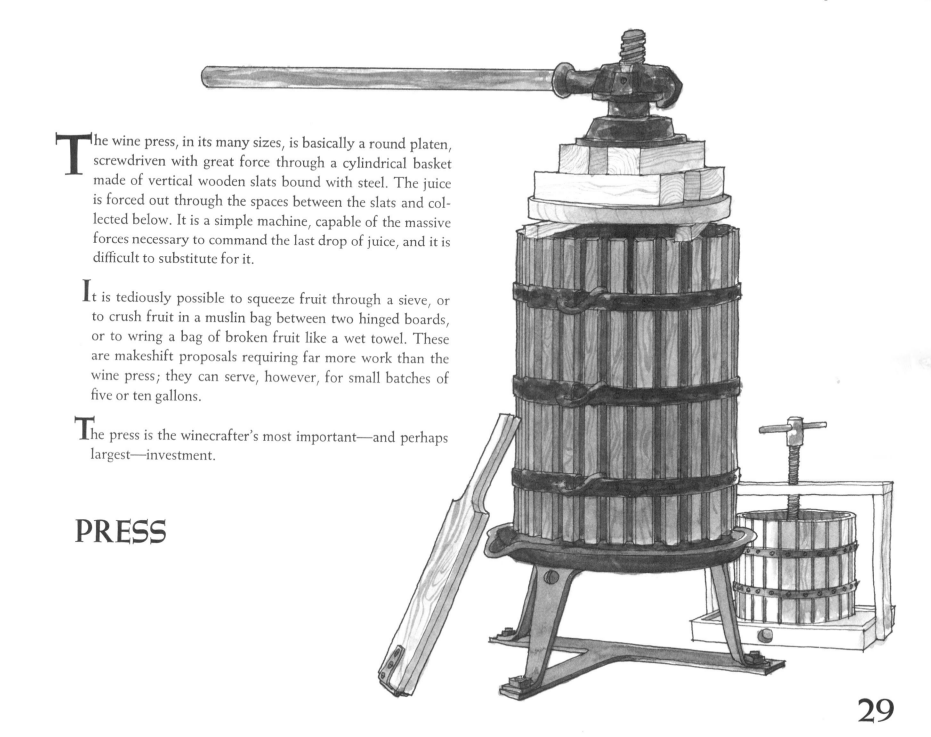

The wine press, in its many sizes, is basically a round platen, screwdriven with great force through a cylindrical basket made of vertical wooden slats bound with steel. The juice is forced out through the spaces between the slats and collected below. It is a simple machine, capable of the massive forces necessary to command the last drop of juice, and it is difficult to substitute for it.

It is tediously possible to squeeze fruit through a sieve, or to crush fruit in a muslin bag between two hinged boards, or to wring a bag of broken fruit like a wet towel. These are makeshift proposals requiring far more work than the wine press; they can serve, however, for small batches of five or ten gallons.

The press is the winecrafter's most important—and perhaps largest—investment.

PRESS

29

CROCKS

Crocks for the aerobic fermentation of red, fruit, and flower wines must be wide-mouthed, nonporous, thoroughly cleanable, and of a capacity at least a third more than the juice and pulp to accommodate the head of foam fermenting will build. It must be possible to stretch muslin or sheeting across the mouth and tie it securely so as to exclude the vinegar fly, which is attracted to fermenting wine almost magically and with heroic dedication to invading your brew.

A good choice is a sound, unchipped stoneware crock. It is heavy and slippery, but is easily cleaned. Some winemakers have recently begun to use plastic wastecans, which present some difficulties. The mold lubricant is not easily washed off and can impart a chemical taste to the wine; plastic picks up flavors from one ferment to another—its surface is more porous than it seems; the quality of the plastic varies, and many factories use plastic scraps, sweepings, and other indefinable bits in their molds—such ingredients are fine for trashcans, but wine is a more delicate charge. If a plastic vessel is the only available choice, scrub it carefully in soda (see *Chemicals*, p. 40).

Wooden barrels or casks are unpredictable, porous, leaky, and troublesome to maintain. They are difficult to obtain (used whiskey or sherry barrels will color and flavor any wine in them) and expensive (decorating ladies are willing to pay more). A clean, sound, charred barrel with its head knocked out is easier to clean and keep if its inner surfaces are brushed with melted paraffin.

Metal, unless enameled, is a poor choice. Metal pickup of only a few parts per million will taint wine. Copper, aluminum, lead, zinc, and iron are especially wicked at pick-up.

Vessels for anaerobic fermentation should be narrow-necked to accept a stopper, nonporous, nonmetallic, and of a sufficient capacity for a ferment—five or ten gallons.

There is one ideal vessel: the glass carboy used to transport acid and dispense drinking water. It is clear, so you can watch the ferment and check the dropping of sediment (called lees), and generally keep an eye on everything. It is cleanable and sanitary. (Acid carboys should be washed *most* thoroughly or the wine will be quite tart.) It is the right size for most batches. The carboy can be purchased at water-cooler companies and through some winemakers' suppliers and some chemical houses. Some may be found at antique shops or decorators' suppliers. The carboy is a standard item of the wine craft.

Perhaps from some lingering romantic notion, a few amateur winemakers persist in using wooden casks and barrels. Cooperage is troublesome, unstable, porous, and unsanitary; it is usually not airtight, and it is opaque. The winemaker can't see what the wine is doing; he must constantly worry about air leaks that will ruin his wine or wine leaks that will deplete it. A barrel takes professional skill and luck to clean it before fermenting and almost supernatural fortune to have it keep without mildewing or cracking between batches. Though some of the great wines have been cask-fermented, assuredly most of the worst have turned to vinegar in wood. Wooden vessels, widely used by professionals, are a risky venture for the initiated, and a foolish choice for the beginner.

While sheet plastic containers are convenient and cheap, they have the same disadvantages as plastic trashcans for aerobic ferment. Plastic laboratory carboys of completely inert material are expensive, but successful.

VESSELS

FERMENTATION LOCKS

The fermentation becomes an isolated microcosm, a small world apart from ours, of yeasts and nutrient. The three major threats to the quiet work of that world are oxygen, internal pressure, and bacteria.

During the first stages of yeast development in the must (the initial mixture of crushed fruit and other ingredients), oxygen is necessary for rapid yeast reproduction, but the second phase of fermentation must occur in the absence of oxygen. The working wine, then, must be stoppered.

Sugars in the wine are converted to alcohol and carbon dioxide in parts roughly equal by weight, producing a great volume of carbon dioxide which could build to explosive pressure in a tightly corked fermentation vessel. The vessel must be fitted with a lock that allows carbon dioxide to escape under pressure and prevents the entry of oxygen. This fermentation lock is among the winemaker's most indispensable tools, allowing the carbon dioxide to bubble out through a water pocket, and effectively excluding oxygen.

Our word for vinegar comes from the French *vinaigre*, sour wine, and any visit to the wine by the ubiquitous vinegar fly (also called the fruit fly) is sure to spoil the wine by introducing bacteria, which convert sugars to acetic acid (vinegar) rather than alcohol. The possibility of contamination from the decomposition of a vinegar fly in the water of the airlock is lessened by dissolving antibacterial sulfur dioxide powder in the water.

The three locks shown here are: an improvised lock made with tubing, a water glass, and tape—it has scant reliability and offers the dangers of spilling and evaporation; a patent plastic lock by Vierka of Germany, efficient and inexpensive; the glass fermentation lock, almost standard for good reasons, the most reliable and workable tool.

Cork stoppers drilled for fermentation locks are porous and should be waxed, if used. Non-porous rubber stoppers are best. Lubricate stopper and lock with water or a drop of antifoam before fitting, and hold the lock in several layers of heavy cloth or a heavy leather glove to avoid serious injury.

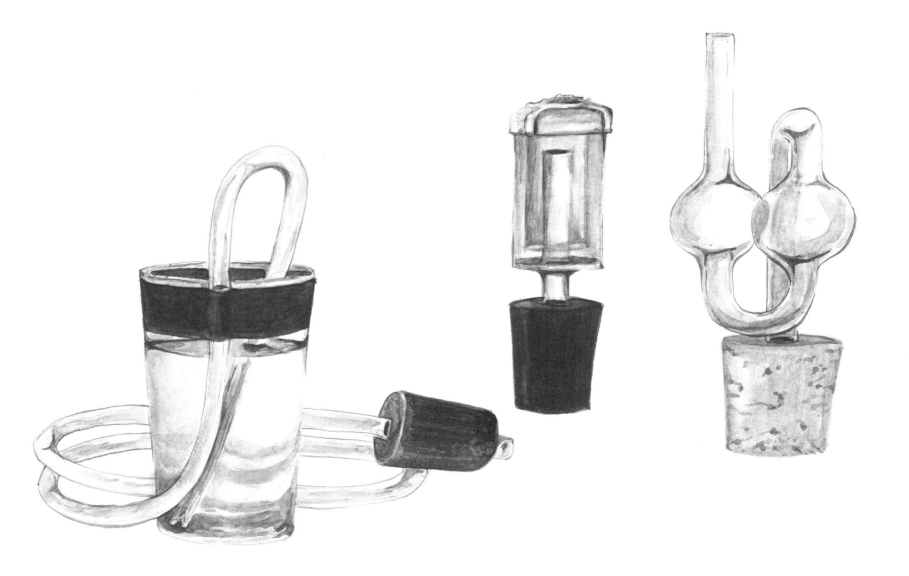

THE HYDROMETER

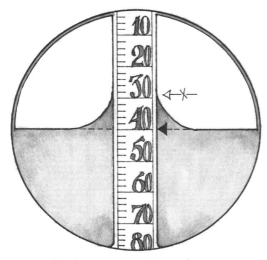

a hydrometer reading of 1.040

A hydrometer works on the principle that a boat floats higher in oatmeal than in water. It measures the density of a liquid by the depth to which its weighted bulb sinks as read along its thin, graduated neck. The system of liquid density is based on water: Distilled water at 59° F. has been arbitrarily assigned a density value, or *specific gravity*, of 1.000. A thicker liquid has a reading above 1.000, lower than 1.000 for a thinner fluid.

The hydrometer is one of the winecrafter's most important tools because of the close relation between a fruit juice's density and its sugar content. Sugar is the predominant factor affecting density, and sugar is the material which yields alcohol in the ferment; if the sugar content is known, then the potential alcohol level may be found, and corrected, with the table below.

A sample of unfermented juice is collected in the narrow hydrometer jar. (Since alcohol is less dense than water, a reading taken after sugars have begun to be converted to alcohol would be inaccurate.) The hydrometer is gently lowered into the fluid until it rests, and is given a spin to cast off bubbles that might affect its accuracy. The reading is taken at the level of the fluid's surface, and not at the height to which the surface tension of the fluid causes it to rise on the hydrometer neck. The potential alcohol level of completed wine can be projected from the reading in the tables. If the potential alcohol level is too low, as it almost certainly will be, sugar must be added to increase it.

A wine with an alcohol level below 10 per cent cannot be expected to keep, and handcrafting methods cannot predictably produce a level above 13 per cent without fortification (the adding of distilled spirits). Between 10 per cent and 12.5 per cent is the range of alcohol strengths in which the winemaker usually works.

Oversweetening is a common fault among beginning winemakers. Excess sugar slows down a yeast culture and can destroy it, and in any case the culture can only convert enough sugar to raise the alcohol percentage to yeast-toxic level. Sugar remaining after that serves to sweeten the wine in a degree difficult to predict. These tables are calculated to produce a dry wine; if a sweet wine is desired, sugar as a simple syrup should be added to the finished wine.

Two specialized hydrometers are: the Busby hydrometer, designed especially for the winemaker and calibrated in potential alcohol as well as specific gravity; and the saccharometer, its name implying its function of measuring sugar content, calibrated in Balling or Brix degrees which equal (for most purposes) percentages of sugar.

As an example, if a fresh juice has a specific gravity of 1.040, it contains enough sugar to yield 5.1 per cent alcohol, or one pound, one ounce per gallon. For this wine, 12 per cent alcohol is desired, requiring a sugar content of two pounds, six ounces of sugar per gallon. Then about one pound, five ounces of sugar must be added for each gallon. Some juice should be drawn off and mixed with the sugar (cane sugar—see *Chemicals*, p. 40). to make a syrup for blending with the whole body of juice. Add this sugar syrup in stages, mixing thoroughly and testing and testing toward the end as the specific gravity is brought up to the 12 per cent mark of 1.090.

In the case of red, fruit, and flower wines, which ferment initially on the pulp and skins of their fruit, such a careful analysis is impossible and the winecrafter must rely on one good sampling and the tables.

A vinometer, shown here, is a simple device for approximating the final alcohol percentage of a dry wine, using capillary action in its thin, hollow neck.

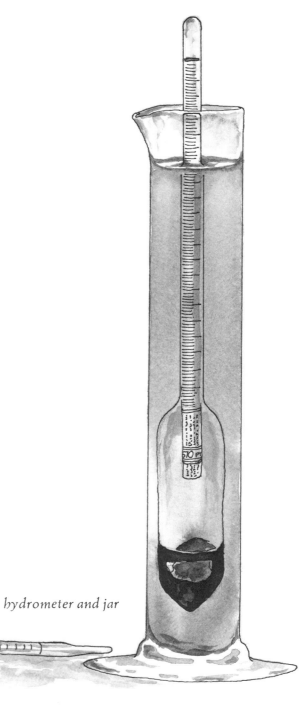

vinometer   *hydrometer and jar*

HYDROMETER TABLES

SPECIFIC GRAVITY	SUGAR PER GALLON		POTENTIAL ALCOHOL
1.020		3 ounces	2.3%
1.030		6 ounces	3.6%
1.040		10 ounces	5.0%
1.050		13 ounces	6.4%
1.060	1 pound	1 ounce	7.7%
1.070	1 pound	4 ounces	9.0%
1.080	1 pound	8 ounces	10.5%
1.090	1 pound	11 ounces	11.9%
1.100	1 pound	14 ounces	13.4%
1.110	2 pounds	2 ounces	14.5%
1.120	2 pounds	5 ounces	16.0%
1.130	2 pounds	7 ounces	17.4%
1.140	2 pounds	10 ounces	18.6%
1.150	2 pounds	12 ounces	19.9%

SULFUR DIOXIDE

Sulfur dioxide is a colorless gas with a strong sulfur smell, used since the scientific revolution as the most important chemical addition to the wine craft. It was first used to fumigate cooperage and to eliminate oxygen in the air space above the surface of casked wines by burning a sulfur candle or a wick saturated with a sulfur solution. Sulfur dioxide combines readily with liquids and assists the wine process in several ways: The hardy wine yeasts are tolerant of sulfur dioxide in strengths that discourage the growth of wild yeasts and bacteria, and so it is a filter excluding harmful organisms; it inhibits the action of the discoloring browning enzymes; it is an efficient antioxidant; it also aids in clarification and in breaking down peel to extract pigment.

It can be considered a poison in strengths far greater than any the wine-maker might use, and even concentrations of less than toxic strength can occasion the unpleasant smell of burnt sulfur, so measurement is important. Concentrations of less than twenty-five parts per million (ppm) seem to be ineffectual, and above 150 ppm might be detectable. A safe range of dosage is 75–100 ppm. The table shows approximate dosages in grams and kitchen measures.

Commercial wineries use sulfur dioxide as a gas or in solution. The wine-crafter can use any one of several dry compounds as a source: potassium metabisulfite (most favored, $K_2S_2O_4$), sodium metabisulfite ($Na_2S_2O_5$), sodium sulfite (Na_2SO_3), sodium bisulfite ($NaHSO_3$), or Campden tablets (which must be tediously crushed to fine powder). Compounds may be ordered from a winemaking supplier, or obtained less expensively from a pharmacist.

⅛ level teaspoon per gallon =	.6 grams/gallon =	75 ppm
¼ scant teaspoon per gallon =	1.3 grams/gallon =	160 ppm
	1.0 grams/gallon =	125 ppm
	1.0 grams/five gal. =	30 ppm

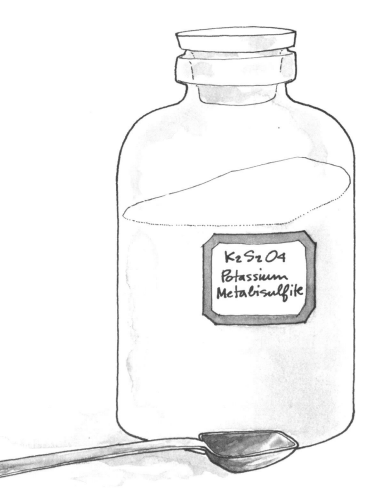

YEAST

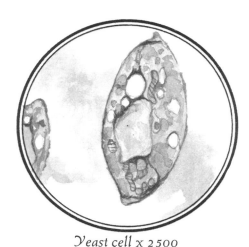

Yeast cell x 2500

Saccharomyces cerivisae variation *ellipsoideus* is the huge name of a very small plant indispensable to the making of wine: It is the wine yeast that converts sugars to alcohols, fruit juice to wine. It is a microorganism requiring fermentable carbohydrates, a defined temperature range, vitamin and mineral sources, and, after a time, the absence of oxygen to do its work. It is really a family of many individual strains valuable because of their hardiness against acid, cold, alcohol level, and other microorganisms.

Wild yeasts of many varieties are present everywhere, airborne. Any of these yeasts will begin a ferment, but few of them are sturdy enough to survive the acid environment of the must (the mixture of juice and ingredients that makes up the beginning wine), and fewer to remain active after they have produced more than 4 per cent alcohol.

In the complex biosphere of a long-cultivated vineyard there is a predominance of proper wine yeasts, and in the past vineyards often allowed these wild strains of wine yeasts to begin the ferment. Today they inoculate their ferments with prepared cultures of known yeasts, as the winecrafter must. The numbers of true wine yeasts on grapes are drastically affected by picking, chemicals, and transport; improper wild yeast may outnumber them. Following inoculation with a vigorous culture of wine yeasts, the prevailing numbers of these yeasts will outproduce, outlast, and finally exclude other microorganisms present in the acid, increasingly alcoholic, cool environment of the ferment, effecting an alcohol percentage of up to 15 per cent and utilizing all fermentable sugars. (A little over an ounce per quart of sugars not subject to ferment will remain.) Just as wild yeasts are not fit for wine fermentation, neither are bakers' or brewers' yeasts; they will ferment insufficiently and impart a yeasty flavor.

Yeast is available in two basic forms: dry yeasts in granular or powder form, sealed in foil packets, and active yeast in a nutrient culture, often agar. Both are available from any supplier of winemaking equipment in a variety of types for whites, reds, champagne, and specific wines. Some dry yeasts require only a half hour or so to become active, bubbling, and frothing, while yeasts in nutrient need a longer time to revive. Any yeast should be started before adding to the must (see *Starter Bottle*, p. 49).

Choose a yeast to suit the type of wine you are making from the supplier's recommendations. Help the yeast to exclude other yeasts and bacteria by keeping the sugar at a proper concentration (high sugar level, as well as high alcohol level, can kill yeast cultures), by fermenting in a cool place, and by carefully keeping the airtight integrity of the vessel.

The grape supplies every need for yeast's growth. Other fruits and flowers, however, must be supplemented with additional minerals, acids, and vitamins. A proprietary yeast nutrient is best (see *Chemicals*).

A yeast culture may become inactive some time before all sugars have been processed. This is known as "stuck" ferment. Fermentation can be restarted by gently stirring up the lees (see p. 57), by moving the vessel into a warmer room for a few days, or, finally, by inoculating the ferment with fresh yeast.

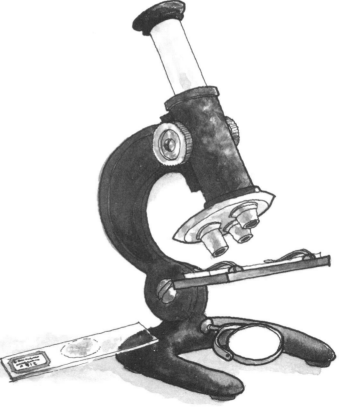

CHEMICALS

PECTIC ENZYMES

Pectic enzymes attack the pectin structure of fruits, increasing juice yield and pigment release. They also assist the clearing of a wine clouded by pectin when natural enzymes are low (as in the case of most fruit wines) or when natural enzymes have been destroyed by heat (as in concentrates). Usually unnecessary for fresh grape wines and advisable for country wines and concentrates, they are available as tablets, powder, or liquid.

YEAST NUTRIENTS

To correct deficiencies in substances vital to yeast growth, most old recipes for country wine included seemingly bizarre ingredients: raisins, lemon peel, malt, ginger, oranges. The grape supplies everything busy little yeast cells desire, but other fruits need additional nitrogen sources, vitamins, and mineral traces. There are several proprietary compounds for use in flower or country wines, or to revive yeast cultures slowed down by cold or high sugar. Nutrients can be measured and handled with greater ease than old additives, and impart no flavor of their own.

ANTI-FOAM

This substance all but eliminates the frothing head of foam on a ferment and may prevent a working wine from blowing through its fermentation lock. It would seem to be a necessity for aerobically fermenting a white wine in its carboy without overflow, and very helpful for other wines. It is completely inert and will not affect taste.

SUGAR

The use of a beet sugar in wine has sometimes caused undesirable flavor changes. The winecrafter should use cane sugar exclusively.

CHLORINE

Dilute chlorine laundry bleach may be used as a disinfectant for bottles, crocks, and vessels, in place of a sulfur dioxide disinfectant solution.

ACIDS

Citric, tartaric, and tannic acids are prime factors in the development and taste of a wine, and are available in convenient forms, but because of the difficulty in accurately measuring acid level in a grape must, and the blank impossibility of estimating it, proper proportions are nearly impossible, and the use of supplementary acids is inadvisable for a grape wine. Some nongrape wines are so deficient in acid, however, that a guess must be made, and a few guideline amounts are suggested with some fruits in *Raw Materials*.

SODIUM CARBONATE

Also known as sal soda, washing soda, and soda ash, this white powder is an ideal cleanser for all winemaking equipment. It is mildly disinfectant, it softens the wash water, and leaves no taste (as does detergent).

CLEARING AGENTS

Traditional substances such as eggs, eggshells, fish scales, blood, and mica are just too messy to contemplate. There are good proprietary agents easily available if artificial clearing is required (see *Clearing*, p. 68).

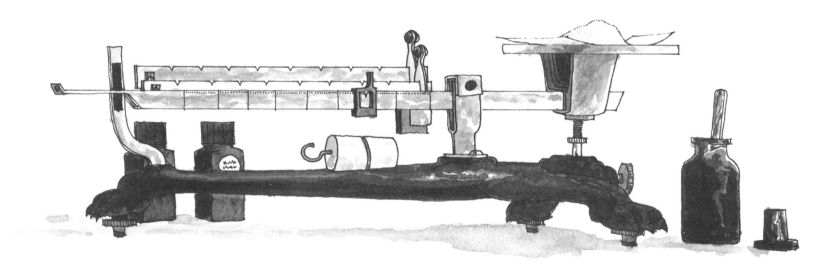

BOTTLES

Wines rest and grow in the bottle; the bottle is a sanctuary, resisting the decaying attacks of oxygen, vermin, and light. The ideal bottle is sound and thick, of sufficient size, designed to be corked, shaped for easy handling, and made of dark glass. The most important requirement is that the bottle be clean.

Thin or cracked bottles are sometimes an awful disappointment. The long care given a wine can be squandered when a bottle breaks during bottling or handling. The sanctuary must be a strong one.

Vintners in all the world's wine regions have settled on bottle volumes around twenty-five ounces as optimum. That amount of wine is a convenient module to accompany two people through a dinner, or three people—perhaps four—through one course. It is a small enough amount to be drunk before it loses its peak. It is an amount large enough to take the air-filled neck space of ½″ to ¾″ without spoiling. In a smaller bottle the neck space would be greater in proportion to the smaller wine volume and would influence it more.

The seal of the sanctuary is the cork, an airtight barrier more efficient against the shocks of our hostile environment than any screw top or mechanical stopper. The cork is driven forcefully into a neck that must be of a size to accept standard corks, and of a thickness that resists the considerable stresses of driving and possible internal pressure from delayed fermentation (always present with sparkling wines).

The standard Bordeaux, Burgundy, and Rhine bottles are strong, stack well, and handle easily. The slim Rhine bottles are too tall to stand in most refrigerators, but their grace compensates for this small inconveniece. Fancy bottles stack poorly, and will not fit some wine racks. The flat, round Portuguese bottles take an odd-sized cork, difficult to obtain. Round Chianti bottles also take an odd cork and will not stand without their basket base. Champagne bottles, strong and easily handled, take only champagne corks fitted with a special corker.

Sunlight changes wine. It can affect the flavor of any wine, and may bleach or cloud the reds. Bottles should be made of dark glass to block out strong light.

Generally, then, the winecrafter should have a stock of Bordeaux, Burgundy, or Rhine bottles of dark glass, taking a standard cork. Beer bottles, soda bottles, screw-top bottles, and whiskey bottles are worthless to the winemaker. Fancy bottles, splits, and bottles taking off-size corks are undesirable.

Wine bottles are difficult to buy. A very few suppliers stock them, and shipping is expensive. If you plan to make wine, you should save the commercial wine bottles you (and your friends) have emptied. After they are emptied they should be promptly washed *without detergent*, allowed to dry, and stored with their original cork—washed—loosely in place to exclude dust, spiders, and other visitors. Just before refilling, the bottles should be rinsed with near-boiling water.

Detergent is harsh and persistent. Its flavor lasts through interminable rinsings, and will devastate the flavor of any wine. Wash with sal soda (see *Chemicals*) and rinse upside-down to remove completely all trace residues. Rinsing by running water into an upright bottle is not at all efficient; filling and emptying take too much time. A stream of water directed up into the bottle with a tube or shampoo hose rinses quickly and completely.

CORKERS

There must be hundreds of configurations for this one purpose. The cork must be compressed and driven into the neck just below the lip. The two models here represent both basic methods of compressing and both methods of driving.

The wooden model drives home with a simple plunger, beaten by a wooden or leather mallet. The cork is compressed as it encounters the narrowing throat below the entry port.

The metal dandy compresses its cork with a cam-action closure when the handles are brought together, and the cork is driven home by a levered plunger.

Corks and corkers work more smoothly if wiped dry before each use.

Corks appeared early in the 17th century as an ideal closure for wine bottles. All tree bark contains some cork, but not in the quantity nor of the quality of the cork oak in Spain and Portugal, which furnishes over half of the world's supply. Cork is strong and forgiving; it will faithfully steward a wine for a century if properly set and handled.

Corks are porous; they retain a trace of wine after the bottle is opened, in a perfect and almost unassailable retreat for growing molds. It is foolish economy, then, to reuse corks. The wine craftsman should use fresh, new corks.

Very few sizes of corks are available, only those that fit standard bottles (number 9 is the nominal size; see *Bottles* for cautions about off-sized necks). They should be of high-grade cork, straight-sided, beveled slightly at the shoulders, and at least 1½″ long. Though they may be boiled to soften them for driving home, overboiling may deteriorate them rapidly. Soaking for a few hours in boiled water and a pinch of sulfur dioxide powder will also soften corks.

CORKS

MISCELLANEOUS

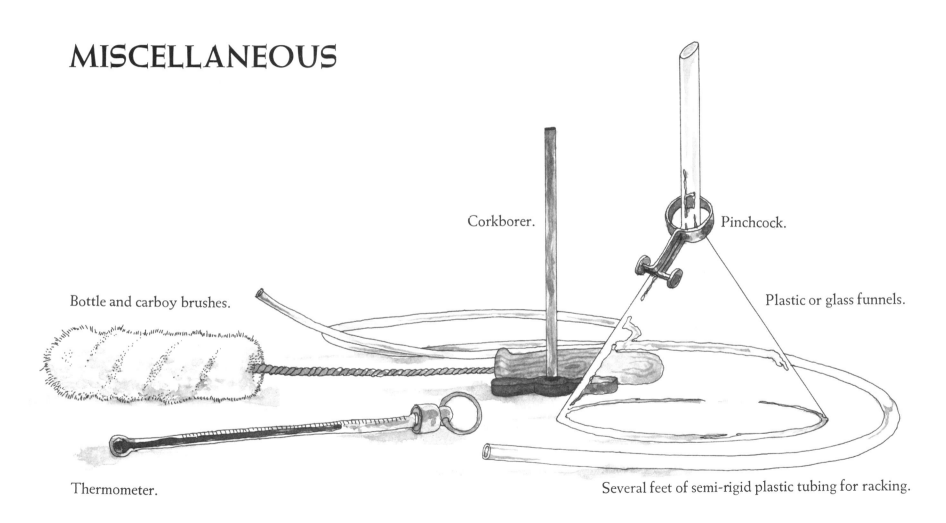

Corkborer.

Pinchcock.

Bottle and carboy brushes.

Plastic or glass funnels.

Thermometer.

Several feet of semi-rigid plastic tubing for racking.

THE MAKING OF RED WINE

BUYING GRAPES

Winemaking is seasonal; you will buy and begin in the fall. Grapes or pressed juice are bought as fresh as possible (though there are a few exceptions to this rule) to maximize sugar content. Rotten or withering fruit is of no use to the handcrafting vintner; it has passed its fullness, its taste is changing drastically, and harmful molds have invaded it. Figure between twelve and fifteen pounds of grapes for each gallon of pressed juice.

If you use liquid yeast in test tubes or agar slides, or if you use slow-starting powdered yeast, it is advisable to give it a running start on reproduction in order to add a large and active culture to the new juice. A few days before you plan to crush grapes, make up a starter bottle: Boil a cup of juice (grape juice or a citrus juice) and allow it to cool in a sterilized bottle stoppered lightly with sterile cotton. When the juice and bottle are certainly at room temperature (temperatures exceeding body heat might destroy the delicate organisms), add the yeast, an ounce of sugar, and yeast nutrient (see *Chemicals*), restopper, and allow it to ferment in a warm, dark, dry place. It will be apparent when the culture is active, frothing, and bubbling. Replenish the juice with fresh juice if the seething slows down before you add this culture to the wine must. Powdered or granular yeast often need only a half hour in a little lukewarm water to revive and begin their work. Consult supplier's directions.

STARTER BOTTLE

WASHING

Authoritative sources are contradictory on the subject of washing grapes. It seems best to rinse the grapes in flowing or at least changing water, picking them over to remove stray leaves, twigs, and rotten, shriveled, or broken grapes. Removing the stems is a time-consuming chore, and the stems do not seem to affect the taste of the wine. Leave them on unless you have Biblical patience. After washing, let the grapes dry for a time.

CRUSHING

Into the hopper go the washed, inspected grapes, the handle turns, the cogs intermesh with a grisly sound, and the juice and pulp for this red wine tumble into the crock for aerobic fermentation. Some winemakers press the pulp now, then mix the pressed juice and depleted pulp together again for a time.

HYDROMETER TESTING

For this batch we will draw off and filter through a sieve only enough juice to fill the hydrometer jar. The juice is tested for specific gravity and its sugar content is found in the tables with the potential alcohol percentage. The amount of sugar needed for the desired alcohol percentage is computed, and the juice used for testing is reserved.

ADDING SUGAR AND YEAST

The sugar is measured and mixed with the juice used for the hydrometer testing to make a syrup which is stirred into the juice and pulp. The starter bottle of recently activated dry yeast is added and mixed.

Ferment begins; the yeast is multiplying its number frantically during this initial stage of ferment in the presence of oxygen. A few drops of anti-foam dispense with the head of foam that may run over the rim of the crock. It is during this primary ferment that vinegar flies are most attracted; hordes appear from nowhere. The crock must be covered to exclude them. Cheesecloth is too porous; a double fold of muslin or, better, sheeting is tied over the head of the vessel like a drumhead. The best tie seems to be a noose (like the bowline shown here) through which the opposite end slips, is drawn tight around material and crock, and secured with two half-hitches behind the noose. Violent aerobic ferment will last up to three or four weeks, bubbling and seething. Aerobic fermentation is complete when the ferment has quieted; most of the sugar will have been converted to alcohol and a hydrometer reading at this point should approach 1.000, or the density of water.

AEROBIC FERMENTATION

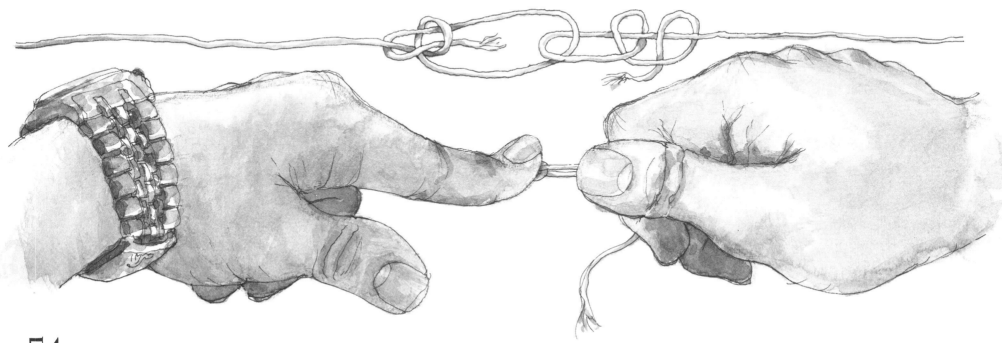

PRESSING

When the ferment has quieted, pressing may begin. The crushed, fermented grapes have lost their slipperiness and will press easier now. Fill the press basket and screw down the platen, allowing the juice to run directly into a carboy dosed with 75–100 ppm sulfur dioxide (see *Sulfur Dioxide*, p. 37). Remove the platen, stir up the "cake," and press again. The bits of peel and pulp that will be pressed into the carboy are an advantage to a red wine, coloring and flavoring through the anaerobic ferment.

ANAEROBIC FERMENTATION

The wine begins. When the juice has been pressed into the carboy, add a few drops of anti-foam and stopper the vessel with a fermentation lock, allowing very little headspace. Fill the bowls of the lock with water and a few grains of sulfur dioxide powder, lightly stopper its exit tube with a bit of cotton, keep the lock filled and the stopper tight. Leave the wine, now—let it build.

STIRRING LEES

This wine has begun in the fall. It ferments in a cool (55°–70°), dry, dark, quiet place, slower and slower until the only sign of action is the displacement of the water in the tube of the fermentation lock. Sometime around the first of the new year, the vessel should be gently agitated to stir up the ugly lees (sediment at the bottom) and so activate any latent fermentation.

57

The easiest and best way to clarify wine is to let it stand undisturbed to throw its own lees, or, drop its suspended sediment to the bottom. The clarified wine is siphoned into a fresh carboy, leaving sediment behind, a process known as *racking*. If the wine was started in the fall, anytime before spring is fine. Patience makes a wine. The fermentation vessel and subsequent vessels should be kept at a height, so that they can be racked without disturbing the lees. A clean carboy with a 25–50 ppm charge of sulfur dioxide is placed below the fermentation vessel and a length of tubing, notched at the upper end to prevent stoppage against the side of the vessel, is started near the surface of the ferment and gently lowered as the level drops. The object of racking is to exclude the fine lees : Be delicate about this operation; do not bump the vessel or try to siphon too near the sediment. At the lower end, the wine should not be allowed to splash to the bottom or run down the side of the vessel, since this aeration would oxidate the wine, affecting taste and color—siphon directly to the bottom and keep the lower end of the tube under the surface of racked wine.

RACKING

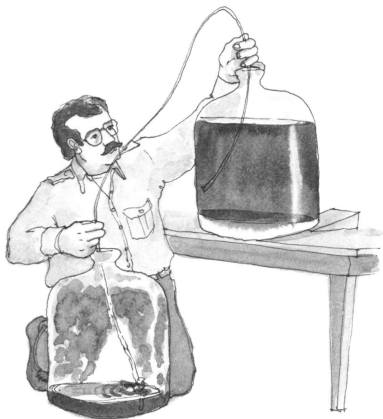

TOPPING OFF

The loss of sediment and the last bit of wine just above it will reduce the volume of the racked wine. To keep air space above the surface to a minimum, the new vessel should be topped off with finished wine of similar characteristics.

RACKING AND BOTTLING

Generally, racking should come after a change in the wine, and a change will come with the change of seasons. Rack when the weather warms for spring, when spring turns to summer, and finally in the fall. Deciding when to rack is a matter of broad judgment. If at all in doubt, waiting a week or two will not hurt the wine. By the final racking the wine ought to be quite clear, ready to be siphoned into a fresh, undosed carboy for bottling. Ready dry, sterile bottles and start a siphon-tube with a pinch-cock shutoff. Fill the bottles to within ½″ to ¾″ of the cork in groups of four or five, then cork quickly to reduce oxidation.

CORKING

Soften new, clean corks by boiling or soaking and drain thoroughly before using. Driving in the cork will be easier if the cork and corker are wiped dry before each operation. The top of the cork should be slightly below the rim of the bottle's neck. It is important to keep all the bottles upright for about a week to allow the corks to set; otherwise the soft corks might be pushed out by the weight of the wine against them.

STORING AND SAMPLING

Wine is a living thing; it receives shocks, and it heals. The shock of racking and bottling has shaken and oxidated it; test it a couple of weeks after bottling when it has restored itself. Storage for a bottle wine is much the same as for a building wine: a cool, dry, undisturbed place away from harsh light where the temperature remains fairly constant.

A mold may appear on the corks of some bottles, or the bottled wine may throw a small amount of lees. Neither occurrence is a calamity, nor will it harm the wine.

Wine ages in the bottle; it sleeps and grows. A long aging does not, however, assure a good wine—it reaches a peak and drops away from it. Some wines should be drunk young, some want to grow more slowly, and there is no fast rule save that whites reach their peak far sooner than reds. Only your growing experience as a winecrafter can tell you when a wine is blooming. Sample a bottle at intervals and record your reactions in a cellar journal.

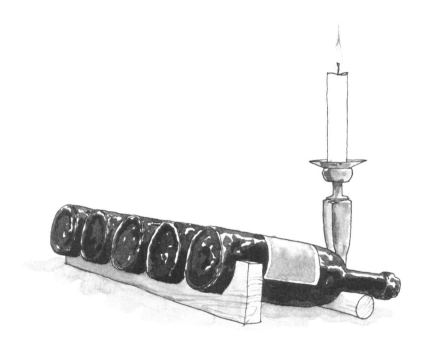

RESUMÉ

The making of a red wine is similar to the making of any wine. The juice of a fruit is inoculated with a strain of yeast in a controlled environment, sugar in the juice is converted to alcohol and the carbon dioxide precipitated is allowed to escape, suspended solids settle to the bottom and are excluded by siphoning clear fluid into fresh containers and, finally, the wine is bottled to age.

And so making wine is really quite simple, is it not? As simple as painting a landscape: a canvas is prepared to receive oils, paint is applied. No, then, it is not simple, the art of the matter is missing. Where is the art? It is in your head and hands; the art of making wine begins in an imagination sensitive to delight. A book can only present the Craft of Making Wine. The choices of methods and materials, the shadings of balance and judgment of timing are your tools, the medium of an art. When you discover that you can make good wine, then you will aspire to create great wine.

WHITE WINE

The making of a white wine does not differ in principle from the making of a red; the differences are matters of timing and, certainly, raw materials. Red wine is made from the juice of red-fleshed grapes—like Foch, Baco #1, Pinot Noir, or Cabernet Sauvignon. White wine is made from the light-fleshed grapes—the Chardonnay, or native Catawba and Delaware, and the Seyval Blanc are a few. The peels of dark grapes steep in and ferment with the juice of the grape to surrender their pigment, acids, and body for a red wine, but the juice from a light-fleshed grape for a white wine ferments alone.

White is the feminine gender of wine; treat it gently and surely. It is more delicate than red wine; overhandling or utensils not antiseptically clean will more readily damage the soundness of the final product. Reracking, an overdose of sulfur dioxide, or a clumsy siphoning may affect its balance.

CRUSHING AND PRESSING A WHITE

Even the skins of light-fleshed grapes can impart pigment to a white wine if allowed to lie broken or with the juice for even a short time. It is important to crush the grapes and press them immediately. In the case of some champagnes admired for their crystal clarity, the crushers and presses are brought out into the vineyard to avoid the possibility of broken grapes on the way to the chateau. A lapse of only an hour or two could blush the wine; crush and press as soon as possible.

Press directly into the carboy for a white wine. The wide-mouthed aerobic fermentation crock is used for a red wine to ease handling of the pulp, peels, and stems, bothersome bulk which is absent in the first ferment of a white wine. Remember to leave some volume above the must for the violent aerobic fermentation. This may necessitate fermenting a gallon or more in a separate jug and adding it to top off before the anaerobic ferment. A cotton stopper or two thicknesses of sheeting can be placed over the mouth of the vessel. Some winemakers place a fermentation lock on at this point, relying on anti-foam to keep down the head that might otherwise push through the lock, and on the vigor of their started yeast culture.

The bits of peel and pulp that find their way into the anaerobic fermentation vessel when pressing for a red wine are all to the credit of the wine's color and flavor, and will settle out. It is best for a white wine, however, to be pressed into the carboy through a sieve to strain out particles that might offer pigment.

Grape juice for white wines, especially the juice of the Delaware and Catawba, may have to be thinned with water, or *ameliorated*, to dilute overabundant acids. There are acid-testing kits and devices for winemakers, but those inexpensive enough for the amateur seem to be inaccurate enough to discount. Delawares and Catawbas can be diluted in a ratio of four parts juice to one part water (see *Raw Materials*).

Water is added in the form of a simple syrup: a mixture of cane sugar (see *Chemicals*) and water in a proportion that tests to a specific gravity indicating the potential alcohol yield desired for the wine. If the wine should have a 12 per cent alcohol content, one gallon of simple syrup with a specific gravity reading of 1.091 is mixed and added to four gallons of juice.

When water becomes a larger part of the wine's volume, its quality becomes more critical. Heavily chlorinated city water, mineral-tainted well water, or rusty tap water can ruin a white wine. If your water is not pure (remember that you may have grown accustomed to its peculiarities) you must find another source.

AMELIORATION

OXIDATION AND TEMPERATURE

The white wine's more delicate balance increases its liability to normal wine hazards. It is particularly vulnerable to permanent browning due to oxidation, and every care must be taken to reduce its exposure to air. Careful racking and bottling without splashing or jostling is important. One supplier offers a pressure siphoning device that lessens contact with air, and it is possible to reduce exposure to some extent during racking by loosely packing the necks of both carboys with clean cloth or paper towels.

Temperature changes, especially sudden changes, can temporarily or permanently cloud a white or red wine. Storage of working or resting wines must be in an evenly cool place. Great cellars are below ground level to take advantage of the natural chill and the averaging influence that raises the temperature gradually a few degrees in summer and relinquishes a few degrees—slowly—in the winter.

CLEARING

A working wine—that is, a wine still actively fermenting—looks hopeless: It is an opaque, moving mass of muddy fluid and foul goo, bits and pieces of suspect matter swimming past; it is obviously not fit to drink and never will be; it may not be safe for external use. The same process that transforms ugly ducklings and buck-toothed girls into swans and Ledas works at this unappetizing muck for several seasons; it clears and refines itself.

The best clearing agent is gravity. Suspended particles, if undisturbed, will settle to the bottom as lees to be excluded in the racking. Almost all wine will clear by settling, some more readily at low temperatures. But the wine craft is not a science, it is an art, and there are stubborn wines that pout inside a peevish cloud. When you have given the wine plenty of time to redeem itself (rack again and try to wait it out) or if you are unbearably impatient with it, you can force it to clear.

Clearing agents have been used for centuries and are used today in many forms: egg whites, toasted egg shells, blood, gelatin, and hundreds of others. Generally, a clearing agent collects suspended particles and drags them to the bottom. There are several good proprietary agents available from suppliers, powders and granules to be poured into the carboy and gently swirled (not shaken) with the wine. Rising and falling, these preparations will collect particles and clear the wine. A cleared wine should sit for several weeks before being racked to bottle.

Clarity is essential to a colorless white wine, and a clearing agent may be warranted. Though an agent may clear a red wine, it may also bleach it, producing an aggressive rosé.

FILTERING

All commercial American wines are cleared by filtering to attain their characteristic brilliance. The filtration systems are large and complex, forcing new wine through filter material with considerable force in an oxygen-free environment. A few vineyards rent the use of their filter to winecrafters; if you are near such an obliging place, filtration may be practical. Filtration by methods normally available to the amateur winemaker is, however, generally inadvisable.

Filtering new wine through laboratory filter paper is slow, incomplete, and invites thorough oxidation. Filtering through whipped asbestos pulp shares the same disadvantages and offers the additional danger of loading your wine with asbestos pulp, an excellent way to cancel out months of work and waiting. On anything but a large, commercial scale, filtration is a bad risk.

ROSÉ WINES

Commercially, a rosé is made by allowing crushed fruit to ferment for a short time before pressing, or by crushing and pressing immediately, but pouring the juice back into a vat with pulp and peels to ferment long enough to capture the blush of color from them. These are procedures requiring the nicest sense of timing learned from long experience.

For the wine craftsman, the second method of fermenting on the pulp is more workable, since he can judge the increase of red pigment easier in juice than in crushed fruit, but it is still a delicate judgment, a matter of only hours, difficult for the beginner to gauge.

The great commercial rosés are made from Tavels, Grenache, or the Gamay strains (see *Raw Materials*), grapes especially cultured for rosés. The amateur can produce an excellent rosé by handling red-fleshed grapes, usually used in red wine, in the manner of a white wine, crushing and pressing immediately to yield a pink juice to ferment without pulp or skins. This method is by far the easiest, and the wine it produces is excellent. It is also possible to blend a red and a white.

THE COUNTRY WINES

It may be superfluous to point out that the grape is not a strawberry. It is important to note, however, that the growth of a grape is critically dependent on a narrow range of rainfall, temperature, growing season length, and soil factors; wine grapes grow in very few regions of the world. It was inevitable then, given the culture-basic use of wine, that a diverse body of nongrape wines should utilize native fruits and even vegetables. These are the country wines.

Country wines are fermented in much the same ways grape wines are, with the same equipment. They are popular with winemakers outside proper vineyard areas, especially in Britain and North-central Europe, and favored by home winemakers because of the availability of raw materials at all seasons.

The disparity between country and grape wine procedures is a function of the grape's willingness to become wine: Other fruits give up their juices and flavors less willingly and are not as generous in supplying sugar and nutrients. A few additional techniques may be helpful in creating fruit wines.

This section concentrates on differences in the handling of grape and country wines. The stems and leaves of non-grape fruit must be removed as completely as patience permits. The fruit must be washed with greater care than the grape. Some vegetables should be peeled (see *Raw Materials*), but skin, peel, and rind should, for most country wines, be treated as in a red wine and used to add flavor, color, and body. After washing, large seeds or kernels (as in apples for wine, cherries, or peaches) are removed, and large fruit is diced.

Greater juice yield, increased color pickup, and easier pressing are possible if the fruit is fermented aerobically with its pulp after crushing, just as with a red wine. Twenty-four hours aerobic fermentation at about 70° is recommended for most fruit. Add sugar, yeast, water, sulfur dioxide, anti-foam, nutrient, acid, and—importantly—pectic enzyme at this point. The enzyme breaks down cell walls, and softens up the structure of sometimes persistent fruit. Sulfur dioxide dosage is the same as for a grape wine.

Some yeast culturers insist that varying yeast strains will vary the finished wine. It is doubtful that any great flavor difference is possible using different yeasts. Judiciously use yeast supplier's recommendations, aiming at a potential alcohol content between 10 per cent and 12 per cent. Use only enough sugar for a dry wine and add sweetening to the finished wine if it is warranted.

Country wines do not age particularly well; they should be enjoyed young.

Press into a carboy, remove the platen and stir up the "cake," sprinkle with water, and press again. Fit the carboy with a fermentation lock and ferment anaerobically through several rackings, using a fining agent if necessary.

There are books listing pages of "recipes" for grass wine, pencil-shaving wine, soap chip wine, and goat hair wine. Though it is certainly possible to set the forces of fermentation to work on almost any organic substance, really only a handful of fruits yields a refreshing beverage. Wine is so much more a process than a conglomeration, that endless lists of detailed recipes for every possible wine are only overstatement and probably inaccurate, calling for definite amounts of sugar without definite hydrometer analysis, indefinite amounts of questionable nutrient, and a sizable overdose of folklore. Crafting wine is not painting by the numbers; the winemaker needs an acquaintance with the fruit, his hydrometer, and one of only a few basic handling techniques, and perhaps the experience of a failure or two to create.

CIDER

Until well after the turn of the century, America's national drink was cider —not the sticky-sweet autumn novelty, but a healthy, hearty, heady, year-round drink for all times of the day and all occasions. Cider making was an essential part of rural America's fall chores, using the best apples and the most massive wooden machinery of the day to turn out a clear, dry beverage of between 8 per cent and 13 per cent alcohol. It was not simply apple juice fermented; an important step took place before pressing.

Round, clean apples, carefully inspected, were first milled in either a grindstone mill or a knob mill resembling a grape crusher but made entirely of wood, into a thick pomace called *cheese*, which was left for a time exposed to the air in order to brown up and lose water in its bruised state. The cheese was then scooped onto mats of rye straw, which were laid in alternate cross grains into the basket of the tremendous press (some cider press oak beams were two feet square) and relieved of every drop of juice. The juice was fermented in white oak casks, and ready to drink in six months.

For today's winecrafter two points are essential: apples with a sufficient acid level, and a strong press to extract all possible juice. Without a press, the cidermaker must content himself with apple wine, to which he adds water (see *Raw Materials*). Winesaps are excellent; bitter cooking apples are good. Wild apples are most flavorful and aromatic. Gravenstein, McIntosh, Northern Spy, Rome Beauty, Spitzenburg, Stayman and Yellow Newton varieties are satisfactory. The Delicious is a poor cider apple.

Start cidering with sound fruit, without bruises or worms; wash carefully, especially carefully if the apples may have been sprayed. Chop the apples and run them through a grape crusher or bruise them with a potato masher. Take a juice sample for a specific gravity reading and calculate the amount of sugar needed for a potential alcohol content of around 12 per cent, but do not add anything until the "cheese" sits in a cloth-covered crock for twenty-four hours. Press the cheese into a carboy with yeast, sugar, nutrient, sulfur dioxide (50–100 ppm), pectic enzyme, and anti-foam to ferment aerobically until violent ferment quiets. Fit the carboy with a fermentation lock and ferment in a cool place (40°–60°) at least six months. Cider aficionados do not rack.

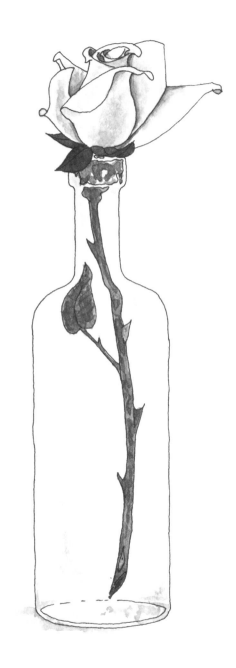

FLOWER WINES

Flowers are an unwilling subject for a wine; they offer little help in producing any ferment, body, alcohol, or taste. Everything necessary for a proper must is added, and even then a flower wine must be bullied into giving up its widow's mite of flavor and bouquet.

Pick flowers (see *Raw Materials*) in full bloom when the sun is up and the dew is gone. Almost all flower wines are concerned with petals alone, which must be separated from buds, stems, leaves, pistils, and insects. Blanch the petals to release flavor and bouquet by bringing several quarts of water, into which the petals have been stirred, to a full boil. Let cool, add enough water to fill a fermenting vessel, and test for specific gravity with a hydrometer. Add the proper amount of cane sugar as a syrup mixed with the flower water. Most traditional wine "recipes" call for a lemon or raisins as a yeast nutrient, but a commercial yeast nutrient may be more easily managed and accurately measured.

Since pectin is not prevalent in flower petals, no pectic enzyme is necessary to break down its structure. Add yeast to the now nurtured must and proceed as with a red wine, to ferment the must with petals aerobically for four or five days. Fit the vessel with a lock and ferment anaerobically through two or three rackings before bottling. Flower wines are at their peak when still young.

CONCENTRATES

Blends of concentrated grape juices for making red or white wines are available all through the year, by mail, from several suppliers. Certainly something of the grape's elusive character has been lost in blending, dehydrating, jugging, storing, and shipping, but some nobility survives these humiliations and an agreeable table wine can be fashioned from the concentrates.

There are not a great many varieties in concentrate form: basic reds, whites, and rosés for table use. After water is restored in recommended proportions the juice can be handled as fresh-pressed juice and fermented as a white wine might (whether the concentrate is red or white, since there is no pulp or bulk involved). Pectic enzymes may be recommended to supply the enzymes lost in heating.

Mix concentrate and water thoroughly, and take a specific gravity reading to determine the amount of sugar to add. Draw off enough juice to make a syrup with the sugar and mix. Since the aerobic ferment will be quite violent, headspace must be left in the vessel (unless you have added anti-foam); a gallon or more is withdrawn and fermented separately. Just before the fermentation lock is set in place for anaerobic fermentation, the gallon is used to top off the vessel. Subsequent rackings and bottling are carried on as for any wine.

SPARKLING WINES

Under pressure, carbon dioxide liquifies in a fluid, and when the pressure is released it expands within the fluid as bubbles. Carbon dioxide is the fizz in soda, beer, and champagne. It is introduced to soda as a gas under pressure, but is generated within the champagne bottle as the result of a final ferment. The fermentation of sugar, you will remember, ideally produces alcohol and carbon dioxide in quantities roughly equal by weight, and half the weight of sugar in the must will account for a huge volume of expanding gas, resulting in a pressure no bottle could safely contain. Though carbon dioxide is now added to pasteurized beer, it was originally introduced by bottling the beer just before the ferment was complete, leaving only enough gas to pressurize the bottle after capping. Champagne and other sparkling wines are allowed to ferment out to a still wine (they are usually blends), and just before a cork is driven in and wired to their thick-walled bottles, a small amount of sugar is added, inducing a final fermentation. This ferment will generate carbon dioxide, and will also throw additional lees which must be removed before aging. Classically, champagne is stored with necks sloping down, and each day each bottle is given a quarter turn and the angle of slope is increased. In time the sediment has collected around the cork. The final step in the making of a classic sparkling wine requires a highly skilled technician, the *dégorgeur*, who freezes the neck of the bottle in iced brine to set a frozen plug between the wine and the sediment. He then removes the cork quickly, blowing the lees out of the bottle ahead of the plug, measures a bit of sugar into the bottle, and replaces the cap immediately, wiring down the cork again.

Of course, technology rampant has devised a method of handling the final ferment with fewer steps and less skill: Inexpensive sparkling wines are fermented in huge pressure vessels and drawn off into individual bottles for marketing. A wine so manufactured must bear the notation "bulk fermented" or "Charmac method."

For the amateur, making a sparkling wine is difficult, requires special equipment, and is just a little risky. It is definitely not an experiment for the beginner.

A detailed account of the amateur process can be found in Wagner's *American Wines and Winemaking*. In outline, a sparkling wine begins with a sound, dry, white wine (or a blend), slightly acid and mildly astringent. Add between 2 and 2½ ounces — no more — of sugar in a simple syrup for each gallon, inoculate with an active culture of champagne yeast, and cover to begin an aerobic ferment for twenty-four hours, or until you are certain the ferment is active. Siphon into clean champagne bottles (the thick walls of the champagne bottles will have to withstand considerable pressure; they should be inspected for faults), leaving about 1½" of headspace, and stopper immediately. Crown caps (as for soda and beer bottles) may be safer for this first capping, popping off before pressure can burst the bottle, and in any case these potential bombs should be handled from this point with leather gloves and safety glasses or a face shield. Lay the bottles on their sides for a long, cool, undisturbed rest; a year is not too long. At the end of a year, turn the bottles end up, almost perpendicular, and give each bottle a lightly jarring quarter-turn daily (this technique is called *remuage*). In a month or more, the sediment will have collected around the cork and it is time for *dégorgement*, or the removal of the lees. Gently place the bottles in a freezer until a plug of ice forms in the neck behind the lees, hold the bottle at a 45° angle away from valuable people or expensive china, upcap and let the ice plug blow the sediment out, *Zut allors!* Quickly pour in about a half ounce of brandy to quiet the wine and top off with simple syrup, cork with a champagne cork, wire it down, and set your vintage away to age through a revolution or two.

CORKSCREWS

The inner workings of a Swiss chronograph are not so complex as some of the machinery devised for pulling a simple cork out of a simple bottle. Here are several simpler models.

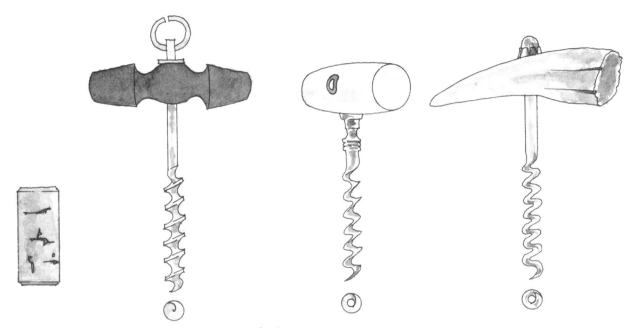

The critical consideration in choosing a corkscrew seems to be the screw construction. Solid-core screws enter the cork like a wedge and may split it. Hollow-core screws of twisted flat stock with edges cut the cork so that it may break. A hollow-core screw of twisted round stock is best.

Gaining mechanical advantage from gears, screws, and levers, these models may or may not avoid flying corks, bottles, and winestewards at that delicate moment when the cork and bottle part.

Failing civilized methods of drawing the cork, this tool retrieves a cork that has been forced into the bottle.

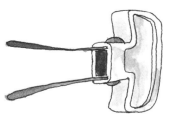

A simple solution: the prongs are inserted between cork and neck by rocking the handle, and the tool is turned as the cork is drawn.

waiter's corkscrew

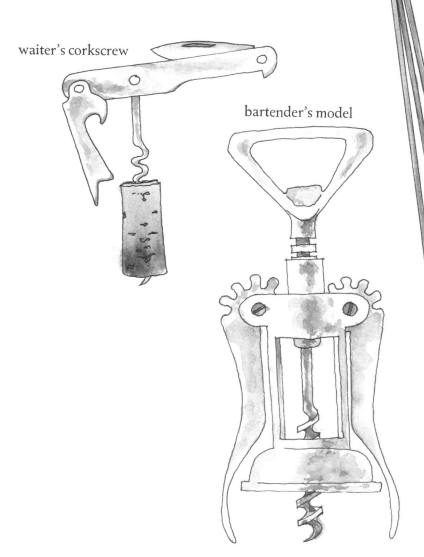

bartender's model

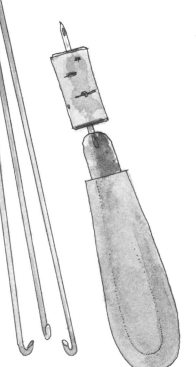

the unlikely but effective "Zig-Zag"

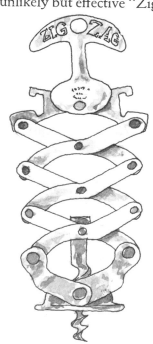

Old corks grown crumbly respond well to this pressure pump. The needle is moistened and pushed well through the cork, the handle is rapidly pumped and pressure builds within the bottle, forcing the cork out. This should not be used with fancy or oddly shaped bottles, which might burst.

The law is clearly in favor of the winecrafter. Federal law permits the head of a household to manufacture up to two hundred gallons of wine each year for his personal use, provided he register his intent five days before he begins with the Assistant Regional Commissioner of Alcohol and Tobacco Tax. He will be required to fill out a cost-free and fairly painless form, Form 1541. You are not permitted to sell your wine, nor to give it away . . . so reads the law, at least.

Cider must be a very patriotic drink, for no form at all is required to make "noneffervescent cider produced by the normal alcoholic fermentation of apple juice . . . without the use of preservative methods or materials."

The production of beer is prohibited without an expensive license requiring safety measures, inspections, retirement funds, and an honest face. Though beer is simple to produce, the government has ruled it an illegal act.

Distillation or simple possession of any unregistered still for any purpose is a great crime against the state, and to be avoided.

The federal laws pertaining to wines are simple and direct: Register, wait five days, and make wine to drink at home with family and guests, but don't sell it, don't even give it away. The dense brush of individual state laws, however, is too wide and too thick to treat here. No state forbids the making of wine, but it is best to consult the tax service of your state for local details.

LEGALITY

Register: Form 1541, Internal Revenue Service.

Family head may make two hundred gallons of wine.

Cider may be made without registering.

Do not make beer, ale, porter, or stout.

Distill nothing.

Consult state laws.

ACCESS

Semplex of USA
Box 12276
Minneapolis, Minnesota
55412

The Winemaker's Shop
Bully Hill, RFD #2
Hammondsport, New York
14840

Aetna Wine Supplies
708 Rainier Avenue, South
Seattle, Washington
98144

E. S. Kraus
PO Box 451
Nevada, Missouri
64772

Milan Laboratory
57 Spring Street
New York, New York
10012

The Country Winemaker
191 RFD #1
Mattapoisett, Massachusetts
02739

Nichols Garden Nursery
1190 North Pacific Highway
Albany, Oregon
97321

Presque Isle Wine Cellars
9440 Buffalo Road
North East, Pennsylvania
16428

There are hundreds of dealers in winemaking supplies all over the country and, certainly, abroad. These domestic suppliers have a broad catalogue of tools and materials.

INDEX

access   88-89
acids   41
aerobic ferment   38, 54
amelioration   66
anaerobic ferment   38, 56
anti-foam   40

bottles   42, 43, 60

champagne   10
      see "sparkling wines"
chemical process   22
chlorine   40
cider   76-77
clearing agents   41, 68
concentrates   80-81
corkers   44, 45, 61
corks   10, 32, 44
corkscrews   84-85
costs   20
country wines   17, 72-75
crocks   30, 54
crusher   28, 51

fermentation locks   32
filtration   69
flower wines   16, 78
fruits   27

grapes, red   25
grapes, white   26

history   8, 9, 10
hydrometer   34, 35, 52
hydrometer tables   36

legality   86-87

nutrient, yeast   38

oxidation   67

pectic enzymes   40
press   29, 55

racking   58
red wines   14
rosé wines   13, 70-71

sal soda (sodium carbonate)   41, 43
sodium carbonate   41, 43
sparkling wines   10, 17, 82-83
starter bottle   49
storing   62
sugar   40, 53
sulfur dioxide   37

tasting wine   19, 62

white wine   12, 64-66

vessels   31

yeast   38, 39, 53

The Grape that can with Logic absolute
The Two-and-Seventy jarring Sects confute:
    The subtle alchemist that in a Trice
Life's leaden Metal into Gold transmute.

Ah, my Beloved, fill the Cup that clears
TODAY of past Regrets and future Fears—
    Tomorrow:—Why, To-morrow I may be
Myself with Yesterday's Sev'n Thousand Years.

Rubáiyát of Omar Khayyám